The Lost Sheep

Written by
T I N A   L O R I C E   C R A Y T O N
Illustrated by
S T E P H E N   A D A M S

AuthorHouse™
1663 Liberty Drive
Bloomington, IN 47403
www.authorhouse.com
Phone: 1-800-839-8640

First published by AuthorHouse 5/10/2010

ISBN: 978-1-4490-7707-5 (sc)

Library of Congress Control Number: 2010906222

Printed in the United States of America
Bloomington, Indiana

This book is printed on acid-free paper.

authorHOUSE®

The Lost Sheep

Written by
TINA LORICE CRAYTON

Illustrated by
STEPHEN ADAMS

The sheep called a meeting in the barn. They talked about their future. "You know it's time for us to leave" said the oldest brother. "We can't stay here forever" said the youngest brother. They all agreed, but were afraid knowing what had happened to their friends years ago. Most of them were eaten by the wolf.

The youngest brother was so excited. "Yes! Finally! I can do what I want to do. I can stay up as late as I want and I can buy whatever I want. No one can tell me what to do." So he decided to look for his own place. He saw an ad in the paper that said "House for Sale." The price was right so he decided to buy it. He furnished it with the nicest furniture and then he moved in.

The partying began. Invitations were sent to all of his "so called" friends. On the top of the list was the wolf. Yes. Can you believe that? He thought the wolf was cool. How soon we forget. He loved hanging out with the wolf. The wolf was invited to come over when ever he wanted. Well what he didn't know was that the wolf was watching him. He was waiting to make his move. "No need to huff and puff to blow this house down. I'm already in," thought the wolf.

While everyone was partying, the wolf was stealing. He stole whatever he could carry. By morning the youngest brother noticed that he had been robbed. He cried "Who could have done this? I trusted all of my friends." John 10:10 says: The thief comes only in order to steal, kill and destroy. So beware of the Wolf!!

Several sheep from around the neighborhood were also at the party. They knew right away that it had to have been the wolf. Would you trust a wolf???? When the sheep realized the wolf's purpose they all scattered and ran off. The wolf was on the prowl again, and this time he had a taste for sheep.

The oldest brother saw it all. He decided that he had to re-evaluate his own friendships. He didn't want to go through what his family and friends did. He knew he had to make much wiser choices. So he decided to look for a true friend. He wanted a friend that he could trust and depend on. That's when he heard about Jesus (The Good Shepherd)

The shepherd takes care of his sheep. He looks for those that are lost or scattered. He helps to heal them when they are sick or hurt. He feeds them when they need food. He doesn't eat them.

On that day, the oldest and wisest brother decided to choose Jesus as a friend. What he didn't know was that Jesus is the greatest friend that you can have. With Jesus in your life you'll always have someone to guide you; someone who will never leave or forsake you, and someone to lean on. On that day, he knew how to live happily ever after until death, knowing that after death comes a new life with Jesus Christ…

LaVergne, TN USA
30 June 2010
187973LV00001BA